UNKNOWN LULLABIES

LAKSHAY SINGH

Copyright © Lakshay Singh
All Rights Reserved.

ISBN 979-888555248-6

To the one's

who left

stayed

staying

Contents

Foreword	*vii*
About The Author	*ix*
Preface	*xi*

Sing Them To Me

1. Energy	3
2. Melancholy	4
3. Quite Days	6
4. Sick Of You	8
5. All My Love Is Free	10
6. Bleed The Same	12
7. Lost With You	13
8. The Interview	15
9. Endorphin	17
10. Kindred Spirit	19
11. Some Sort Of Art	21
12. Childish Sense Of Pride	23
13. Love Like Alexander's	24
14. Not A Love Show	26
15. Struck By None	28
16. Unknown Lullaby	29
17. Him	31
18. Inseperable	33
19. Sweet Relief	35
20. Family Reunion	36

Contents

21. She   38

22. They Could Have Been   40

23. Waste It Carefully   41

24. Cry Of An Angel   42

25. Beach Boys And Girls   44

26. Movie Screens   46

27. Insomnia   47

28. Trying (always Will)   49

29. When You Are Not Here   51

30. Alone Not Lonely   54

Bonus Content

31. Beloved Brother   59

32. Nonsense   61

33. You Are Enough, I Have Got You   62

We Will Be Alright   65

Foreword

This journey of ours is sometimes too sweet and sometimes as cruel as falling into a gutter on a Sunday morning. This journey of ours is sometimes as beautiful as a woman in her wedding dress and sometimes as ugly as the bullies can be. This journey of ours is sometimes as high and drunk on a new year's eve and sometimes as dull as a mirror on a December evening. This journey is cruel, insightful, hopeless, extraordinary, sorrowed, sensual, happiest (maybe not), proudest, and the most unique. This journey is what we call the complicated and fucked up story of one's life.

I know your grandmother used to sing those melodious lullabies when you were not able to sleep or whoever used to sing those peaceful, calming lullabies when you wanted to doze so badly. It can be anyone who can sing you lullabies or maybe sing a song to you. This book is a song or maybe call it a bunch of lullabies but they are not sung by your grandmother. These are the lullabies of life, these songs are sung to you by your own life. Life is a bitch but she sings well precisely.

This book might be a savior for someone. These lullabies are a savior for me sometimes and a fucked up girlfriend to me some nights.

Don't worry this will not do you any bad, i am here to save you because i was not.

- lakshayy

About The Author

LAKSHAY SINGH is a student studying in high school currently. "Unknown lullabies" is his second official book.

He published his first official book called "Midnight ecstacy, midnight sorrow"
He released poems on social media as an interest in poetry and then decided to take this hobby on a professional level.

Preface

I wrote a bunch of thoughts, a bunch of emotions. Two years ago I was not doing good. I was not stable as a young teenager, no teenager is stable though. My heart wanted to say yes but my brain stopped and called it quits. I had no idea who I was. Just a regular high school teenage guy aka bro trying to cope up with his studies and matters of the brain and that thing called heart at the same time. No aka bro it is not easy but we all go through it and somehow face it and finally get out of it.

We as teenagers feel a lot like aka bro a lot. As I said before I was not doing perfectly as I should a few years ago but it's okay. It gets better I promise. But yeah until it didn't, no it was not sweet at all.

This book is filled with everything I could have felt and every heartbeat I wanna portray as a confident teenager. I am happy now and it gets happier I promise again. In the end, everything's going to be alright

okay?

promise me

Sing them to me

1. Energy

You don't have to worry
There is nothing to hurry
I won't last
I loved you for the last time
My energy won't last
Old poor heart of yours
I know about your all fours
This won't last
I touched you for the last time
My energy won't last
Visions you are lost in
Like a deal, you always win
This Deal won't last
I wrote about you for the last time
My energy won't last

2. Melancholy

A heart made of glass
You can see right through it
Do you feel the sensitivity
Please try not to break it
It has gone through a lot
So it's grown delicate
With a bunch of thoughts
It is tender to touch
It cried in the night
It felt sorry for itself
It went dull for a time
Like deep in the end
At the end of the caves
To control its emotional behave
This heart hates getting emotional
Don't wanna let them know
They seem happy with the other side
And I never tried
To make them bear with this go
Why would I let them know?
This heart cries and cried
Teardrops like raindrops
Said went to the bathroom

But cried loud as much it wanted too
Tried itself to heal up the wounds
It always tried to love more
Don't wanna cry melancholy
But tears poured

3. Quite days

I don't feel the need
Sometimes I am lonely
Sleeping by the books
I don't feel the greed
An avidity to get hooks
It feels alright
Sometimes to be alone
There are no mind games
Gathering myself to make love
Not in the love of names
Read a book
Listen to music
I am not bothered
Nor I am cupid
But maybe
On these quite days
Without any chase
Of the human race
I feel the love
The inner love phase
It feels silent and quite
Which is needed sometimes
Not locked in a room

But giving meaning to myself
Which I may presume
Candlelight and flowers
Gifting to myself
Reading books and feeling the rain
Somedays are quite
And I feel alright
Without any might

4. Sick of you

I know I don't need you
You wouldn't even mind
I have been acting so stupid
After, everything I have left behind
I know I made a mistake
Fell In love with you
Got me into a heartbreak
Got me under the weather
But then,
I know they frighten you
Every time they think that you are in love
But you are not in love
There's nothing good about you
And I know you know,
That you are not delighted
Every time they presume you try your best
You just want me off your chest
All you did was got me messed
No, i will not take more
I know you used to sent me flowers
Used to water them everyday
But when you changed the plot
So now I let them rot

So sick of you
I know I deserved better
But no I will never
Like an open letter
No, I will not,
Get me into something like you

5. All my love is free

Yesterday,
I realised what you have done to me
You came back
Said you were misunderstood
An absentee
Don't you know what you should have done?
How you should have treated me
Empty going on my mind
I was losing me
Like It was all aligned
Made the world fall on me
Can't keep what's holding me
At a sensitive time
I was forgiving the plea
Taking you back
Can things be fixed, Maybe?
But I realised,
What I have been through lately
Gotta hold my own
I don't need an old-timer
Gotta keep that love alone
Needless to be a social climber
You don't have to ask now

A chance I won't respond
I have realised now,
My mind will not allow
Myself has withdrawn
Judas, now we don't belong
I got many others to take care of
You were just heavy on my empty mind
I don't want you, I succeeded
All my love is free and I am free
Endlessly, without forgiving any plea

6. Bleed the same

I put an all-nighter
So, I could love you like the clouds
But carrying a cruel lighter
You burned the clouds with thunder
I just wanted you to come home
Everything was set
Not like a pleasant monochrome
It turned out as a threat
This is not a joke anymore
I love you
No,
I loved the old funky you
We used to get dirty in the sand
Didn't care about our mushed up hands
But now I see someone else
You are somebody else
You don't like the sand anymore
You prefer weed with a nice cigar now
Where is your authentic blood type
You don't bleed the same now

7. Lost with you

There is no need
No need for a decision
To choose a path
Always like a sociopath
I come back to you
I already know what I am thinking
A train to catch
Or a ship sinking
Whatever we take
Without any blinking
I will go with you
All I wanna do
Is to be with you
In the woods, in the ocean
You are my mysterious emotion
I will follow you till the end
Even if it's slow motion
Lets runaway
I want to get lost
It can be a paradise
At any cost
Just take me with you
And let's get lost

We can make a tiny house
House-made of wood
Like they do in Hollywood
Just you and me having time
Without any tension
As if it's some lover's dimension

8. The interview

I know
You don't care about
The interview
In which I talked about
Only you
I can't help it
Because whenever I write
Oh boy, it comes back to you
They kept asking questions
I answered none
And I gave no mentions
I said,
It's just an obsession
Every time I write
You hold back my mind
It's false to take a flight
I know my find
I know my kind
I was in front of the mirror
Thinking
Interviewing myself
Convincing
How to get you off my shelf?

But I can't help it
Silly me to fall in for you
Dilly dilly you made me talking
I love the thought of us in the evening
Makes me wanna believe in love
The way you talk, something about its healing
I know you are the real thing
Tell me what's your point of view
Can I take your love interview?

9. Endorphin

You act

I forget

You speak

I sweat

You call my name

I am all set

My body doesn't know

How to respond to you

I really want to, you know

But when you come through

I ignore all the due

And just happily stare at you

I am not telling you to talk

I am not asking you to speak

I just want you to,

Stay with me

My surrounding feels lonely

Even if it isn't

There is something missing

I work out myself with the vision

That you are here sitting

Listening

When I feel the discomfort

They keep on chatting
Over my head, I don't want it
They are laughing, I am lagging
But when you are around
You held my hand
We just took around
Felt better with you, away
And when I feel down
You sense and sit beside me
An unknown endorphin
I feel around me

10. Kindred spirit

Not the least days I would spend
Every time I look at it
Something called a new way
Make it back to the ashtray
I don't miss the siren sounds
I don't want to lay with the false hounds
What am I missing?
Sipping faded coffee grounds
Walkaway in the quite timberlands
It will have what I need
Just some fresh weed and haze
And some summer blaze
I will feel the drizzle
The unbothered kindred spirit
Black skies raining on me
The river of the pirate
Skinning to the finest
Living in the 21's
I have seen it all
From apartments to that very tall
To the covered in sand beach ball
But with my girlfriend's and boyfriend's
The grassy land's and rainfall's are above all

Locked out of pure heaven
Deep inside
As she said,
Throw away my cellular device
The pirate will show the path
The sun will calm me down at last

11. Some sort of art

This day has been feeling sweet
Apocalypse in the shady rain
I was alone but at least I bought a coffee
Reeling through the midnight streets
I could talk all the good
The people I met, the kids I laugh with
I kept down in front of them, I don't fit in
Point of fact that I don't even want to fit in
They seem alpha, like they would eat me alive
Why should I consider them
All they do is bulk and make fright
Well, I do laughed so it's okay
The writings I do are pleasing me enough
But sometimes all I really think about is you
And I don't even know you, or who to call
I don't even understand
What kind of art of someone
Will please my mind and soul with the glory so loving and
kind
Any drink suggestions because sometimes all I feel is love-
blind
Reeling through the midnight streets
Sipping coffee beans until the loneliness fades

But that will never be enough
Sinking feeling in my heart
It's not okay but is it that tough?
To look at me once, as if I am some sort of art

12. Childish sense of pride

Drinking on that old mountain
You said come with me behind the fence
In that vintage father's jeep
Does it really makes sense ?
I didn't find it cool at all
You parked the jeep in the carry
Said, look at the moon
It didn't felt scary
When I look at your face
My heart ignore the denies
It's my childish sense of pride
Or my fate which applies ?
That sparked gaze in your brown eyes
And those high mountain dew
What are the chances I would cry ?
I won't even stay awake too
To make myself high, look at the sky
I feel love responding to me and you

13. Love like Alexander's

I can't beat the Russian poetry
But I can ample you like Pushkin did
Our love is like some sort of rocketry
Rugged to understand, complicated
But we can set off to Madrid
And forget about the devastated
I will love you like Alexander's poesy
I will hold you like Shakespeare's writings
I will treat you like Jack and Rose's romancing
I will make you fall in deep like the titanic beneath
It is all hard to believe
But you make it profound and leave
Makes me wonder, silly me
Fell in love with a serious creature but a sweet relief
When you are around, your voice
Your voice makes this reality a safer place
I get struck by your words even if they just say
Even if it is too much cliche,
My heart doesn't jump off the cliff, just stays at bay
My lord what's happening to me?
Am I romanticising or being too much romantic
I am not forcing, I am just not holding
This is all natural, a bit of sweetness in this realm

My heart is reciting, without any overwhelm

14. Not a love show

You got that body
Probably gonna run to you
Everyone got your name on their tongue
And I act like I don't know you
You got that accent
I am happy for them
Getting to know an actor
But they don't know how numb
How numb your heart is, made up of a plaster
You got that different glory
A new attitude like a player
But that didn't matter
You look like yourself
But you are somebody else
You look so happy
Left me here betrayed
You treat me with a spade
Even if I made a card
A card handmade
They think you are catchy
What they don't know,
Is how your heart fades
And how your mind will blow

When they stop the loving show

15. Struck by none

What if I need someone greater
I can't hold hands with everybody
Crossing a road is different
When crossing with that certain somebody
I wish I could carve my name on a tree
Yes, I did when I was 8 years old
But now it will be different
Adding the name of someone too close
I watch them at the diner
I keep on watching with some visions
They talk a lot and I can see that spark
That glowing spark in their eyes
My eyes feel dull and dark
Waiting for my surprise
Can't fight these lonely nights
It scares me what if there is no one
What if there was no one
Patiently waiting with life
To not get struck by none

16. Unknown lullaby

Something about you isn't right
Like an old hindsight
Everything was over
I was hurt more than ever
You said you like music
So you played with my heart
Played with my heart like an instrument
Played it hard until it got withered
There were no strings attached
Felt like an old guitar
There was no playing
I missed the melody
Somebody else was it
I didn't even know he was at your door
You both ended up together
End of our Midnight chores
The reckless melodic chores of your lover
Calm and innocent my heart
Just wanted some trustworthy harmonies
But you sing him the lullaby
Lullaby for the baby lover
I loved you but its better
To not see the faded colours

Our melodies will be shaded forever

17. HIM

Remember the stuff toy I gifted you
You have a keychain dedicated to me
It say's,
I feel about you makes my heart lone to be free
I say,
All I want is you with me carefree
I never had the courage to say
Feel like to state it on your face
But then I realise what may
Can cause a wounding misplace
Words I want to say
Voices in the background of my head
Wish I could sing em to you
It would heal all the bled
Heart believes you love me
And my body knows the truth
Live together, los Angeles, California
Wherever with my sweet tooth
Wrote about you a hundred times
Waiting for the real life
Every time I write it's you
Every sign is for you
All the fine lines

Like hopeless navy blue
Be my appreciated crime

• 32 •

18. Inseperable

On those midnight streets

Just the two of us, you got a bit emotive

You don't have that kind of character

Being expressive in your DNA

But when we are alone, your heart tends to sway

It makes me feel comfy

A bit sentimental too

That you utter some of it

I didn't had any clue

You had so much to share and commit

But there will be a day

She will take you away

I will stay comfy if you stay

But I won't make you choose

Between me and your lover blues

Your body will be in her arms

But your soul will rest with me

You can call me when you wish peace

You can ask me when you require advise

Its okay if she cries, you don't have to fall for lies

She knows we are inseparable

Our relation isn't disposable

If she want, she would make you forget

Every moment, every minute we had spent
But I am not a fool nor a threat
She says she loves you, whatever she meant
I will be saving my love for you
I am here for you, without someone's consent

19. Sweet relief

Monday is sour
Exhausted, got me crazy
Wait for it to get over, counting hours
Needy for some flowers, like blue daisy
Stressful are these days
Or is it me without any blaze
Days are getting bitter, so is my life
Want something sweet to taste
To bring the bitter taste to a halt
You passed by me
Beat up the plays
Shakespeare won't have disagreed
You were like a fresh haze
Yes, you made my days sweet
Got me something like a sweet relief
Always stay by my side
Like the blue daisies at the lakeside

20. Family reunion

This is not about my father
Nor about my mother
Not even my brother
And yes not about my dog too
A short love letter to my family
The family without parents
Made me happy and grateful
Like never before
They are like my own flesh
Withstanding life together
Hindsight 2020
I miss you more than plenty
I love you
I love them
I love him
I love her
No matter what happens
I know you are with me
Without any glee
I will trust you and love you
You are my family
You are my lifesavers
Like you were on a mission

To save me from hardening's
Let me tell you now
I have the opportunity
Even you point a gun on me
I know I will keep you closer
I miss you
I love you
To my dearly, friends

21. SHE

Don't match her beauty
She is one of a kind
comparison is futile
Change the state of mind
Her willing soul is not a disability
She doesn't need your crutches
Insisting is not the weakness
You never let her progress it
She is beauty
White as snow, black as a bird
Both are beautiful
Your eyes are just blurred
You don't have to speak for her
She has her word
Words can speak
And it will be heard
Inside she must be crying
Because of you, she was dying
Still, she loved and cared
And she is always prepared
Questions herself if she is worth it
The sweat and tears shredding
And you don't care

Just waiting for her in the bedding
She will comeback
Not like you
Like you being violent
She will comeback
But this time
Not being silent
She can and she will
The inner her is the god
She is a woman
And a woman is a god

22. They could have been

We all are broken and sad
What about the dreams we had
I break down at 2 AM and call
Remembering vegas while alone
Hope a saviour awaits and breaks the wall
We been dancing on these fallen leaves
There must be a solution I might see
But from the phantom and the graves
There is nothing I see
My hopeless words are resting praised
Its not okay to loose, I call it wrong
Love might be pain, but there he goes
Not to blame anyone
Lies his dirty clothes
Then he wiped his toes and slows
Its the end of the telling they do
Comes the starting what you prove
Get caught, don't pretend
They could have been or dreamt about
No such thing as doubt or dream about
Fill the drought and act out, while they shout

23. Waste it carefully

Hold up, my heart call it quits
Honestly it is drowning
After everything was a miss
A subsequent lover
From another, you make it hit
There's no second guessing
If it all dries up, I will be dressing
Still, I will be into it
Saving my love for you
Underneath the sky of blue
Listen,
Won't take more of your time
I just really want you to know
Will be okay if you leave
There in the back you will find me
These clocks are getting old
So, take my love and waste it carefully
I fall to easily
And I have been thinking about you lately
When we are done
I won't take the pain, so just take me in your arms
And break me gracefully

24. Cry of an angel

It's okay too care too much
Good for them, good for their appetite
There's nothing wrong in expressing
Until it's coming out right
It's okay to love too hard
Nice for their brain, pleasant for their heart
At last I adored my best
It was not a test, I granted my part
Their considering, their hands
I am trying to learn by heart
The canvas of my life
How will it turn out?
A pleasant smitten art?
Will I care if there's no rebound
Maybe not
But you will hear the cry of an angel
Abandoned in the meadows
Sobbing with the shadows
An angel
Who always loved, and always tries too
But sweetie pie world is cruel sometimes
Again with a sigh
Heavy in my heart, teardrop in my eye

It's okay to cry
I can be needy too
But my heart's sensitive
Maybe my brain too
I don't know what to do?
Trust me, all my love is for you
Love to make your day, to make it golden
And believe me,
When you try to love me back
I feel cherished, my heart turns molten

25. Beach boys and girls

The time of summer
Got all over my sunny
Beach dreams, tasting honey
Eating cream and spending funny
Wind through my hair
Cold feet water
Me and his daughter
Tiding with the waves
His daughter is my sister
Seeking beach boys together
Like modern architecture
Clicking polaroid picture
Don't know how to surf
So we went to the beach club
Then we soaked up the sun
Sand skinny heat up
Everything went orange
Then it was dark as night
There was a cottage
Full of candlelight
Beach boys and girls were there,
Drinking and dancing
I didn't drink I swear

But yes, I might be romancing

26. Movie screens

Why do you have to worry?

I already booked two tickets

Let us reach out early

I am counting minutes

We take the upright seats

The one in the corner

From those rainy streets

Now, here with you is warmer

They turned out the lights

Now it's only the scenes

I can't wait anymore

Let's dance in front of the movie screens

All I can see is a bench

Look moon is here too

Can you speak French?

Well, je t'aime ma lune

Je t'aime ma lune - i love you my moo

27. Insomnia

I don't like dreaming
If it's not about you
The same old folk tale
Like a halftime show
Every night,
I want it repeating
I don't believe in love
If love is not about you
Like they did in the nineties
Stargazing and no sleeping
Every night,
Even if it is freezing
I don't like sleeping
If I am not with you
Insomnia all night
Needing you by my side
Every time,
Like Bonnie and Clyde
Staying up all night
Beating up poetry
Only romance and dance
Than dreaming of France
Everyday,

We take a chance
One step forward
And no steps back

• 48 •

28. Trying (always will)

Last years were like some mental cages

Trapped and somewhere down staged and sacred

Every step and word was killing me wide

I just want to get well from the inside

Gathered a lot of regrets and lessons

I don't really talk about my depression

But eventually time found it's way

Thankfully I don't hurt and feel the weigh

Every time I write or confess

My mind don't really take a guess

I just wanna keep on working

Working on my heartfelt and wording

I hope you already can take a guess

All I do is try and address

I don't wanna leave and feel

Nor I am trying to be the conceal

Keeping the aura and myself bright

Always trying to be happy and alright

After everything I have seen, and passed by

There is still so much to absorb and deny

But I just want you to know

I am always trying, always will

Life is so cynical but still so beautiful

Navigating myself to a better mindset
Keeping it suitable with some meaningful sweat

29. When you are not here

The winter's coming in
I can feel it at the door
But what's the point of cold
When I do not have you in my arms
Yes, precious you are such a charm
Make those storms go away
Whenever I hear the alarm
My steps to your broadway
I had come a long, long way
Just to have you for the day
But when you are not around
Trust me,
I trip off from my bed
In my hopeless hotel
And I don't speak that well
Because,
when you are not here
All of the hotels seem vacant
No kids playing on the beach
I try my fullest to reach
But how will I finish the unknown
The blind path to the sun
Without the presence of my moon

I hope you hold my hand soon
No,
I love it when you talk
I love it when you walk
But don't walk away
The hotels need you to stay
Doubting at the corner of my bed
Was I made for you?
Do dreams really come true?
Remember,
I can be your sweater
With a warmer hug
To remind you every clock
I will be there
And you don't have to knock
Just get in, our bond is rare
That's what I also say to them
When you are not here
The hotels will be ready with lights
The kids will be swimming at the beach
And you will be here with that stare
Now, I will feel the wintry air
And I will praise the words you speak
Every inch to every speech
You make me not stay in my lane
Fought all the chains
To make a hopeless gain

When you are here
I don't take a look at the pain
You have my heart
You owe my brain
Because,
Now you are here
And now you will stay
Sun and moonlight with the artic wind
Every night and every day

30. Alone not lonely

God it goes up
A whole new regime I am following
Absorbing the sunlight and emitting dreams
I am loving what I am doing
I am happy going to the grocery store for a walk
Being alone really is therapy
What I am saying is, I am not lonely
She is here when I need and him too
But when I find peace in the rain
My heart tells me to leave alone
I don't phrase that, I choose it
It clicks again
I am alone but not lonely
When I am alone I feel more to the ground
spending time alone (it do is therapy)
I am not saying I don't like to socialise
Or I don't have the desire to attend events
of course I want to but,
When I am alone, i am able to present myself out there when
I want to more confidently
It won't ruin my experience because of someone's else
opinions

I am able to create my own opinions and it is calming, well
more satisfying to me
Talking to no one for a hour and gathering yourself (really is
therapy)
I am alone
I like to be alone
I don't phrase to be alone
I choose to be alone
I am not lonely
I am with myself
Gathered myself
Feared out myself
Love myself

Bonus content

31. Beloved brother

Laughing out loud
Over stupid things
An amenity to me
You made living easy
Can't disagree
My kindred spirit
You are one of a kind
Cherish every minute
You are like a fresh wind
Gratefully designed
Kindhearted at it's most
Loves to eat sweets
Let me raise a toast
To remind you
That you set the peace
I love you so much
You can't even imagine
The one who never Judge
Sometimes get's angry
But I still love the way you nudge
Eat, breathe and repeat
Life is incomplete without you
No one can compare and compete

I know, we know
You are a gift it's true
Loved, adored, and admired
My beloved brother
The one we all desired
We love you
More than any other

32. Nonsense

I have always dreamt of something that isn't true
I wanna give power, gain power too
Really, I was hard at it to catch
Now I adore the perfect match
It was all nonsense back then
I don't regret the previous times
Well it got me the opposite
It was like reading between the lines
Now I don't lack any of it
Better and higher
The standing ovation was satisfying
They and I are proud, I admire
Messing up with extract, got me stoned
Crying got in my blood
Bleeding every day for previous hours
But now I don't think of that
Well, now they send me flowers
I am loved in the after hours

33. You are enough, I have got you

I didn't realise until now
My mind was full of difference
Now I made it to fix it
Now I know where to sit
You don't have to speak
I can see it in your eyes
The vow we want between us
I can feel it without the discuss
Love is not enough
But at least I have got you
Got your touch
Got your sweet nudge
I won't
And I don't
Regret your much less
At last, it was all a stitch
I am happy I know your address
I am alright with the progress
Quite not what I imagined
Best way to show 'I love you'
We can't be too chatty
But I will still keep you happy

I will stay and wait for you

I will not force you to stay

I will miss you badly

But you know

You will find me in that old alley

You are enough

I will stay right here

I love the way you smile

Until next time with you

I will wait in the meanwhile

We Will Be Alright

You are enough

You are worth it

You are strong

You got it my love

I promise

www.ingramcontent.com/pod-product-compliance
Lightning Source LLC
Chambersburg PA
CBHW031328130726
47988CB00007B/3030